CW00394819

The town of Lavenham was the centre of the Suffolk wool trade from the 14ᵗʰ to the 16ᵗʰ centuries. Edward III (1327-1377) had granted favourable terms to encourage Flemish weavers to come to England. Many settled locally and set up a flourishing business. Shilling Street commemorates the Schyling Family, one of the original group. During the reign of Henry VIII (1509-1547) the town was one of the richest in England. Trade began to decline towards the end of the 16ᵗʰ century with the introduction of water powered fulling mills; weavers migrated to areas like the West Country where water power was more readily available. Lavenham was never again as wealthy, the sumptuous timber framed Halls, Merchants Houses and cottages were never replaced or updated leaving us with a splendid legacy of distinctive medieval architecture.

The 141ft high tower of the magnificent church of St Peter and St Paul, completed early in the 16ᵗʰ century at around the same time that the guildhall was built, dominates the town and is a landmark for many miles around.

Kentwell Hall (walk no 4) was built by William Clopton during the 16ᵗʰ century and completed in the reign of the first Elizabeth. There have been few alterations since. It is now owned by the Phillips family who have spent the last thirty years restoring the house and recreating the gardens, it is open to the public in the summer months. Melford Hall, close by is a National Trust Property.

Male skylarks mark their territory and attract mates with their distinctive birdsong delivered in flight. They inhabit vast open fields and will not be seen until they rise up suddenly from the ground the song cascading around. They flutter higher and higher, the sound still distinct until the bird cannot be seen against the sky. The song will stop abruptly as the bird dives down and disappears again easily within crops or stubble.

We feel that it would be difficult to get lost with the instructions and map in this booklet, but recommend carrying an Ordnance Survey map. The walks are on Explorer Maps Nos 196 and 211; Landranger No. 155 covers at a smaller scale. Roads, geographical features and buildings, not on our map but visible from the walk can be easily identified

1   The Hobbets

5³/₄ Miles   3 Hours

Drive north on the B1115 out of Hitcham and turn left at the first junction toward
Cook's Green and Brettenham, after about a third of a mile park in the wide
entrance to a bridleway. No facilities. **Muddy in wet weather.**

1   Start along the bridleway away from the road and follow the right hand edge of
the field with the hedge to the right. Go through the hedge gap, turn right at the
signpost through the trees and turn right at the exit by the marker post at the seat.

2   Turn left on the grass track over the field and turn right at the signpost along
the right hand field edge, the bank slopes away to the right. At the next signpost
go right through the field entrance and then left to regain direction with the dyke
now to the left. Keep going past a footbridge, turn left over the stream at the
wooden rails and turn right. At the signpost go through the gate and keep direction
to the road between the pink and the white houses to the road. Turn right.

3   Turn right again at the 'White Horse'; turn right into Bury Road across the white
railed bridge. Turn immediate left along the left hand field edge, just before the top
corner turn left over a footbridge marked by yellow arrow discs. Turn right along
the farm track and left over the footbridge with handrails.

4   Follow the arrowed direction over the field ahead; this field may be under
cultivation but a path should be well marked within any crop (if the track is
indistinct, it bears right halfway up the hill towards the large house).

5   From the house the path can be difficult to follow but goes to the marker post
on the left of the small wood to the right. Walk past the marker post on the left
hand side of the field, turn left over the footbridge and right to regain direction. Go
through the hedge gap in the corner, cross a white stile and bear right through the
gate. Follow the dyke on the left into a fenced farm road nearly to the tarmac road.

6   Turn right over the footbridge, follow the fence through the hedge gap and turn
right between fence and hedge. Cross the footbridge and the field beyond in the
arrowed direction towards the wood. Turn left along the edge of the wood and
follow as it bears right; turn left along the grass track between fields. Join the
tarmac road past Castlehill to the road.

7   Continue ahead over the stile slight right and keep along the left hand field edge
past Devil's Hill Wood. In the corner cross the three sleeper footbridge go through
the gate and turn right, follow the right hand field edge to the marker post; turn left
and keep direction along field edges through the farmyard. Go through the gate
and turn left at the sign.

WALKING CLOSE TO

LAVENHAM in Suffolk

Number Twenty Three in the popular
series of walking guides

Contents

Walk		Miles	Page No
1	The Hobbets	$5^3/_4$	4
2	Thorpe Morieux	$3^3/_4$	6
3	Nova Scotia Lane	$4^1/_4$	8
4	Kentwell Park	$5^1/_2$	10
5	Chad Brook	$8^1/_2$	12
6	Shimpling Street	4	14
7	Brent Eleigh	7	16
8	Thorn Corner	$7^1/_4$	18
9	Smithbrook Lane	$6^1/_4$	20
10	Bull's Wood	5	22

Walked, Written and Drawn by Clive Brown

© Clive Brown 2004 – 2020

Published by Clive Brown
ISBN 978-1-907669-23-1

PLEASE
Take care of the countryside
Your leisure is someone's livelihood

Close gates
Start no fires
Keep away from livestock and animals
Do not stray from marked paths
Take litter home
Do not damage walls, hedgerows or fences
Cross only at stiles or gates
Protect plants, trees and wildlife
Keep dogs on leads
Respect crops, machinery and rural property
Do not contaminate water

Although not essential we recommend good walking boots; during hot weather take something to drink on the way. All walks can easily be negotiated by an averagely person. The routes have been walked and surveyed by the author, changes can however occur, please follow any signed diversions. Some paths cross fields which are under cultivation. All distances and times are approximate.

The maps give an accurate portrayal of the area, but scale has however been sacrificed in some cases for the sake of clarity and to fit restrictions of page size.

Walking Close To have taken every care in the research and production of this guide but cannot be held responsible for the safety of anyone using them.

During very wet weather, parts of these walks may become impassable through flooding, check before starting out. Stiles and rights of way can get overgrown during the summer; folding secateurs are a useful addition to a walker's rucksack.

Thanks to Angela for help in production of these booklets

Views or comments?
walkingcloseto@yahoo.co.uk

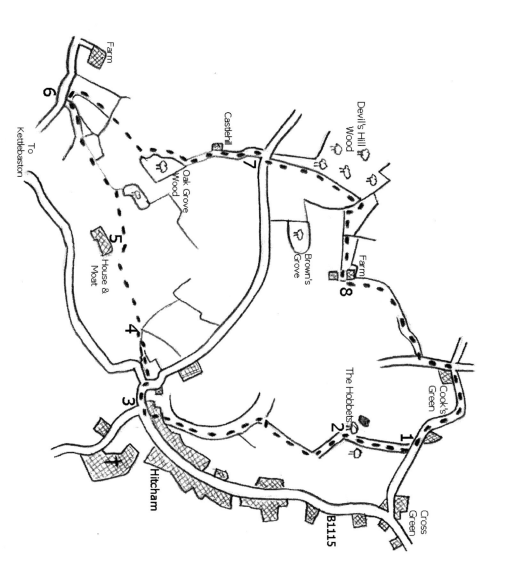

8 Follow the left hand field edge all the way to the road as it bears right, slight left and right again. Turn left up to the crossroads, go down the road right, through Cook's Green to the bridleway entrance and your vehicle.

23:H

2 Thorpe Morieux

$3^3/_4$ Miles $1^3/_4$ Hours

Find a parking space in Thorpe Morieux village. The 'Bull' pub a mile north
of the village on the way to Bury St Edmunds.

1   Walk out of the village north on Bury Road. A quarter of a mile past the village
hall turn left through the gateway at the signpost, turn right then follow the farm
track left between the avenue of trees.
2   As it bears left onto a concrete road, bear right along the left hand field edge
with the dyke to the left and walk up to the road. Turn left then immediate right on
a road and a path between hedges, go through the hedge gap and turn left.
3   In the corner turn right with the hedge on the left up to the marker post, turn
left and enter Bull's Wood through the kissing gate. Take the waymarked path
diagonally right through the trees; at the pond bear left on the path on the edge of
the wood, keep direction along the strip of trees and the right hand field edge.
Continue past two marker posts on the path between the trees and along the
potholed tarmac farm road on the other side of the buildings.
4   As the road turns right, turn left and keep direction on the right hand field edge,
carry on down the narrow track between the trees and the right hand field edge
again. Keep going along the concrete road.
5   At the signpost on the corner of the sleeper walled farm enclosure, turn left and
walk down the hedge lined path. Step right, through a gap at a marker post and
continue with the hedge now to the left. Cross the footbridge and the stile, Keep
direction through the gates across the Llama fields and go over the almost hidden
stile onto the road. Turn left back into the village and your vehicle.

Morieux was the family name of the medieval lords of the manor at Thorpe; the
suffix was tagged onto what is a very common village name.

23:H

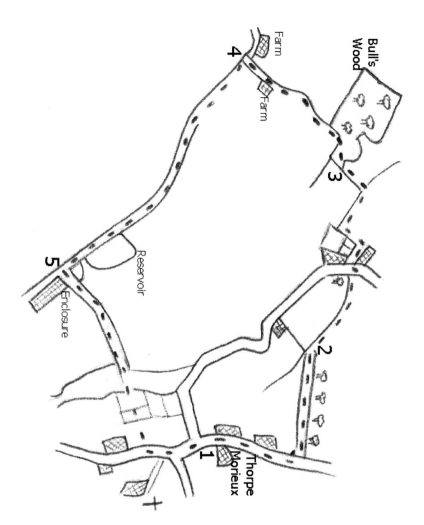

Bull's Wood is mentioned in documents dating from 1279 and is now part of the Woodland Trust. Charcoal burning and traditional woodland crafts are practised here.

The artist John Constable, went to school in Lavenham where he was apparently very unhappy. One of his contemporaries at the school was Jane Taylor who wrote Twinkle, Twinkle Little Star.

23:H

3 Nova Scotia Lane

$4^1/_4$ Miles   2 Hours

Park in Preston St Mary, no facilities.

1 Start along the tarmac farm road left of the church. Continue between the farm buildings downhill on the concrete road. At the bottom of the slope, cross the stile ahead and bear right with the fence to the right. Go through the gap in the trees and turn left with the dyke on the right; cross the footbridge and the stile.

2 Cross the dirt road and the stile the other side, walk uphill on the grass path between the hedge and the fence on the right. Cross the stile at the top and turn right along the road for half a mile into the dip to a footpath sign by a metal gate.

3 Follow the arrowed direction between the fence and the hedge, turn right in the corner past the marker post and continue with the dyke to the left. Keep direction over the drive in the corner turn left over the footbridge, go past the marker post uphill over the farm road and follow the path to the hedge gap and on to the road.

4 Turn right, double back along the road and turn immediate left downhill; go right, around a double bend, past a T-junction and straight on at the Preston St Mary sign along the byway Nova Scotia Lane. Walk past the farmhouse to the signpost on the right.

5 Cross the field which may be under cultivation although a track should be well marked and continue past the marker post with the hedge on the left to the corner. Go through the hedge gap and carry on straight over this field (a path should be visible within any crop), go through the hedge gap down over the footbridge and stiles. Turn left along the road through the settlement of Whelp Street.

6 Just before the road swings left turn right through a gate, then immediate left over a stile next to a gate and follow the field edge right. Continue through the gate on the right of the long narrow field and through the gates at the end along a hedged track. Turn right over a stile and follow this grass, hedge lined path parallel to a farm track back to the church at Preston St Mary.

An **option** in wet muddy weather at point **5** is to carry on along Nova Scotia Lane to the road, turn right to the corner of the road in Whelp Street, but be careful to take the road through the gate around the corner not through the hedge gap on the corner.

23:H

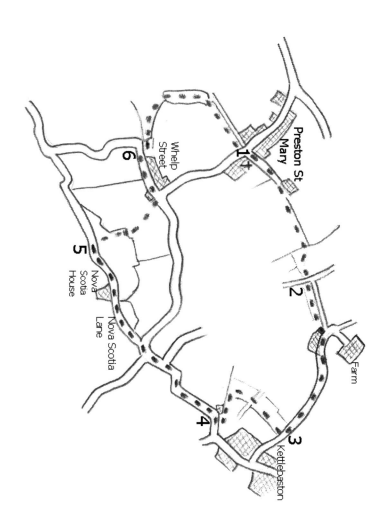

The Guildhall of Corpus Christie on the Market Place in Lavenham was the centre of the local cloth trade. The guild was an organisation protecting the rights of both employers and workers; it set prices, controlled wages and kept rigorous standards in the production of cloth. It also looked after its members in illness and old age. After the guild declined it saw service as the Town Hall and a wool store, but its use as a prison was limited by prisoners being able to kick their way out through the flimsy lath and plaster walls. The Guildhall is now in the care of the National Trust and has displays of local history and the wool industry.

23:H

4 Kentwell Park

5$\frac{1}{2}$ Miles   3 Hours

Park in Long Melford in the car park opposite Melford Hall, toilets at the edge of the green at the top of the hill, pubs, cafes, restaurants and shops in Long Melford.

1 Turn left out of the car park entrance and walk up the hill past the triangular junction towards Bury St Edmunds. Turn right along the concrete road into the garden centre just before the 'Hare', keep direction through the garden centre and out down the tree lined track. Go through the gates and cross the busy A134 Long Melford bypass carefully, keep direction ahead on the right hand side of the field.

2 At the bottom of the slope, turn left and follow the right hand field edge with the trees on the right. Keep direction through the boundary to the corner and turn left. Turn right through the hedge gap at the marker post and almost immediate left keeping Chad Brook to the right. Continue out of the scrub and up to the footbridge, cross and carry on along the other bank and follow the tree lined bridleway to the road at Bridge Street.

3 Go over the bridge to the left, cross the A134 road and walk into the village past the 'Rose and Crown'. At the top of the slope turn right into Aveley Lane. Turn left up the steps by the signpost and continue along the left hand field edge, from the marker post cross the field ahead in the arrowed direction; a track should be visible although the field may be under cultivation. Go through the hedge gap turn slight left and carry on over this field.

4 Turn left at the boundary along the left hand field edge and bear right in the corner to the marker post in front of the wood. Turn right down the edge of Brakes Ley Grove and keep direction with Ashen Grove to the right. In the corner bear right along the hedged farm track and turn left at the junction of farm roads close to the derelict Kiln Farm.

5 Walk down this road to where it swings left level with Kentwell Hall, go straight on over the stile on the right of the road and turn left at the track; continue through the gate and the trees to the right of the gatehouse. Bear right along the lime tree bordered entrance avenue and walk 300yds to a stile on the right.

6 Cross and take the arrowed direction over the field to a stile just to the right of the church, go over and through the stiles and down the left hand field edge. Carry on through the gate, turn left over the stile and go through the rectory garden. Bear right out of the gate and through the churchyard, keep right past Trinity Hospital and walk all the way down the slope to the car park and your vehicle.

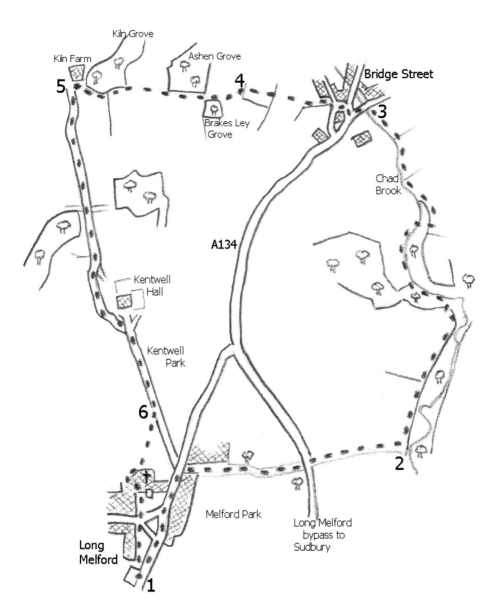

The imposing lime tree avenue leading to Kentwell Hall was planted by Sir Thomas Robinson, a wealthy London lawyer who bought the property in 1676. In 1683 he had to jump from the window of his London office to escape a raging fire. His apparently great weight would not have helped his chances of surviving the fall and he died soon after from his injuries.

5   Chad Brook

8$\frac{1}{2}$ Miles   4 Hours

Park in Lavenham in the car park next to the 'Cock Inn', toilets at entrance, all other facilities close by in the town. Take care crossing the busy A134.

1   Leave the entrance to the right, walk through the town and over the disused railway bridge; turn left down the steps and follow the left hand field edge right then left. Just past the telegraph poles turn right along a track to a signpost, turn left along the right hand field edge to another signpost.

2   Turn right on a short piece of tarmac road, continue ahead on the field edge through the gap. Follow this hedged path right then left; at the signpost bear left over the corner of the field and keep direction over the next field to the marker post. Bear right along this concrete road; 150yds before this road ends turn left.

3   Cross over the neck of the field with the trees to the right and continue ahead on the concrete road again past two junctions and through trees. As the road swings right go straight on along the grass path on the left hand field edge. Carry on right/ahead on a short length of concrete road and turn right down the grass bridleway between hedges.

4   At the end of the path bear left over the field, which may be under cultivation although a track should be visible within any crop, to the right of the cream house. Bear right at the marker post along the gravel drive to the road, turn left and walk up to the A134; cross and follow the road left into the wide layby past the garage.

5   Turn right along the road in the layby signposted to the church, as the hedge on the left ends turn left at the signpost and follow the left hand field edge. Continue to the footbridge and cross; turn left and go along the track with the dyke to the left. Carry straight on over a three sleeper footbridge and stile. Go down the edge of the playing field and step over the stile to the right of the gate.

6   Cross the A134, walk along the road opposite (signposted South Suffolk Route) over the bridge across Chad Brook to the signpost and turn right. Continue between the trees with the brook to the right and then the right hand field edge. Go round a right hand curve through a boundary and turn right at a marker post.

Alpheto

To the Church

Bridg

6

To Long Melford

Chad Brook

Page Twelve

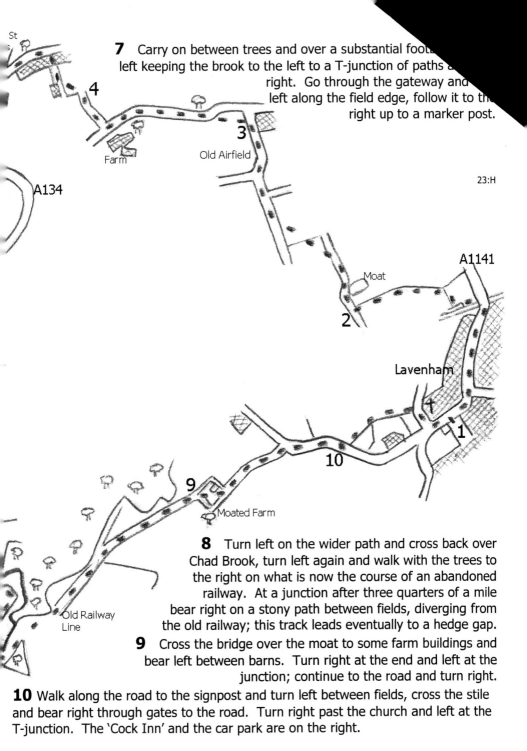

7 Carry on between trees and over a substantial foot[bridge] left keeping the brook to the left to a T-junction of paths [and] right. Go through the gateway and [turn] left along the field edge, follow it to th[e] right up to a marker post.

St

4

Farm

Old Airfield

3

A134

23:H

A1141

Moat

2

Lavenham

1

10

9

Moated Farm

Old Railway
Line

8 Turn left on the wider path and cross back over Chad Brook, turn left again and walk with the trees to the right on what is now the course of an abandoned railway. At a junction after three quarters of a mile bear right on a stony path between fields, diverging from the old railway; this track leads eventually to a hedge gap.

9 Cross the bridge over the moat to some farm buildings and bear left between barns. Turn right at the end and left at the junction; continue to the road and turn right.

10 Walk along the road to the signpost and turn left between fields, cross the stile and bear right through gates to the road. Turn right past the church and left at the T-junction. The 'Cock Inn' and the car park are on the right.

ımpling Street

/iles   2 Hours

Park in Alpneton in the layby off the A134 signposted Alpheton Church. No facilities.

1   Leave the layby heading north on the roadside path with the A134 to the right, to a signpost at the entrance of the rough tarmac drive Nuns Drift. Turn left, past the footpath signpost, down the path with the hedge to the left and the cottage to the right. turn right on the field edge and almost immediate left across the open field which may be under cultivation although a path should be well marked within any crop, to the wide gap at the marker post.

2   Go through and keep direction over the field, a track should still be visible, go through the narrow gap and turn right, with the hedge to the right, into the corner. Turn left up to the corner of Alpheton Hall Wood and carry on through the wide gap and then the narrower gap in the boundaries.

3   Turn right, with the trees still right; continue through the gap between buildings and go down the path left of the barn between the barn and the hedge. Keep straight on to the crossroads of tracks at the signpost; carry on through the double wooden gate and walk up the right hand field edge with the hedge to the right.

4   Cross the footbridge in the corner and carry on up the field edge, hedge still right, through the gap in the corner and continue with the hedge now left. The track goes up the slight slope between fields and ahead to the junction by the clock in Shimpling Street village.

5   Turn right along the street to the footpath signpost on the right and take the path between the hedge and the outbuildings. Cross the two sleeper footbridge at the end and bear left, with the hedge to the right. Go through the boundary and follow the field edge as it meanders more or less straight on, with the hedge still right. Go through another boundary, passing left of the moat in the far corner. Turn left and immediate right across the tarmac driveway.

6   Continue direction through the hedge gap and keep straight on with another moat to the right, to the marker post at the corner of the trees. Take the wide track on the field edge to the right, with the trees to the right, to a farm road. Cross and bear right on another wide track on this field edge, with the trees again right.

7   The trees end at a marker post at a junction with a hardcore farm road. Turn left along this farm road, between the fence and the dyke all the way to the A134.

23:G

8 Cross carefully and keep ahead through the narrow path between hedges to the road, turn right back to the main road and take the roadside path to the left. Cross back with care and follow the roadside path back to the layby to find you vehicle.

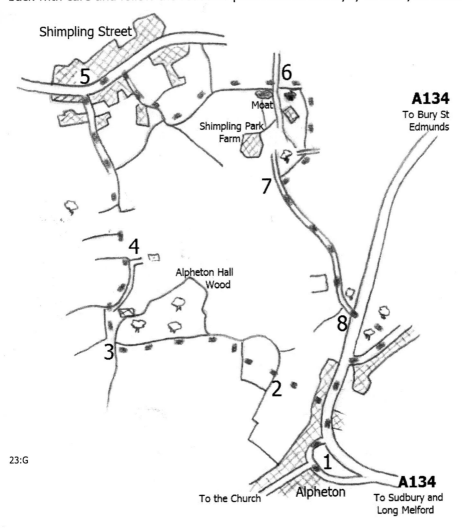

23:G

Despite its medieval appearance, Lavenham has been used very little in films and television series. In the seventies the film 'Barry Lyndon' used the town as a location and parts of 'Children of the New Forest' were filmed here. 1980 saw the making of an advert for the new Austin Metro and in the nineties the town featured in scenes for the antique dealer series 'Lovejoy'. Long Melford also featured in some of the 'Lovejoy' programmes.

7 Brent Eleigh

7 Miles   3$^1/_2$ Hours

Park in Lavenham in the car park next to the 'Cock Inn', toilets at the entrance, all other facilities close by in the town.

1 Turn right from the car park entrance, walk downhill straight on at the junction past the 'Greyhound' and the 'Crooked House'. Turn right into the narrow Market Lane and keep direction through the square past the 'Angel' into Prentice Street; go down the slope to the T-junction. Cross the road and go over the brick bridge, turn left then bear right at the marker post. Carry on up the slope, this field may be under cultivation but a path should be well marked within any crop.

2 At the marker post continue ahead along the left hand side of the field; bear left then right over a dyke to regain direction and keep this direction as it zigzags along field edges. At a marker post go over a sleeper bridge and bear left down a tree lined path to a tarmac farm road.

3 Turn left for 50yds, then right at a signpost over a footbridge and along a field edge with the trees and the dyke to the right. At the marker post turn right over the footbridge, turn left to the next corner and then right; go left around a dogleg in the corner and cross a footbridge ahead. Turn left, right and left; continue over the next footbridge and go down the left hand side of the field. Keep direction along the field edges to the road corner at Whelp Street.

4 Take the road right which leads around the bends eventually to Brent Eleigh. Go over the bridge and fork left along the cul-de-sac. Carry on through the fence gap, over the A1141 and up the road opposite.

5 After 150yds at the signpost go up the steps and along the path between hedge and fence, continue along the right hand field edge and bear left. Turn right at the corner, go through the trees and past the two signposts; maintain direction over the field (a track should be visible within any crop) to the road.

6 Turn left down the slope across the bridge and turn right at the signpost, follow the field edge with the stream to the right. At the concrete farm road turn right for 10yds, turn left at the marker post along the well used track between the hedge and the trees. Bear right on the avenue between the trees and slight right again along the path with the tall hedge to the right. Keep direction past two signposts down a dirt farm road with the dyke to the right

7 At the marker post turn right up the slope, turn left through the first hedge gap and down then right hand field edge. Just short of Bear's Lane Farm turn right at the signpost along the farm road, bear left around the farm to a more substantial road and turn right. Continue down the road past Weaners Farm to the signpost.

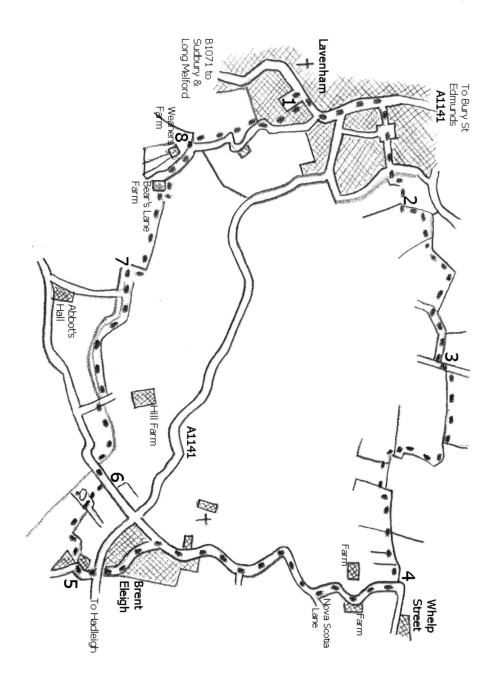

Lavenham

To Bury St Edmunds
A1141

B1071 to
Sudbury &
Long Melford

Weavers
Farm

Bear's Lane
Farm

Abbot's
Hall

A1141

Hill Farm

Brent
Eleigh

To Hadleigh

Nova Scotia
Lane

Farm

Farm

Whelp
Street

1

2

3

4

5

6

7

8

Completed on the next Page (Eighteen)

8   Turn left for 75yds to the marker post and turn right, cross the field to the gap by the house ahead touching the road at the corner by the allotments. Follow the road left/straight on; as it swings right go along the path straight on past the car park. Turn left and left again at the end into the car park to find your vehicle.

---

8   Thorn Corner

$7^1/_4$ Miles $3^1/_4$ Hours

Park in the lay-by off the east side of the A134, a quarter of a mile north of the Thorn Corner junction (signposted to Shimpling). Grid Ref 889536. No facilities.

1   At the north end of the lay-by turn right at the signpost down the right hand field edge next to the conifers, turn right and follow this field edge left. Walk past the first signpost and turn right at the T-junction of paths at the second signpost, with the dyke and the small stand of trees to the left. Keep direction to the next boundary on the left and turn left along the left hand field edge, with a dyke and a hedge to the left.

2   At the signpost by the farm road turn left uphill, bear right between the Dutch Barn and the house. Walk up to the A1141 and turn left along the roadside path. After 200yds turn right at the junction, signposted Cockfield, continue over the disused railway bridge. Turn right, signposted Button's green.

3   As this road veers left turn right at the signpost along the right hand field edge. Go past the signpost and follow the old railway line south for just under a mile and a half. The path on the line ends at a signpost just over a sleeper bridge; turn right along the stony road to the A1141.

4   Turn right for 250yds, then left, signposted Smithwood Green, as this tarmac road swings right, turn left on the concrete road and turn almost immediate right. Follow this old airfield perimeter road and bear left as it narrows. Bear further left and turn right at a signpost past a metal barrier, keep direction past a junction on this tarmac road to the A134, cross and turn right along the roadside verge.

5   Turn left at the junction (Thorn Corner) for Shimpling and follow the road for two thirds of a mile. Just past the entrance to Shimpling Park Farm turn right at the signpost over a 3 sleeper footbridge; cross the narrow piece of field (a path should be visible within any crop). Keep direction over the boundary along the right hand field edge; bear right at the top right field corner and follow the stony, then tarmac farm road bearing left between the farm and the house.

6   Turn right at the green triangle junction, walk up to the A134 and turn right the short distance to the lay-by and your vehicle.

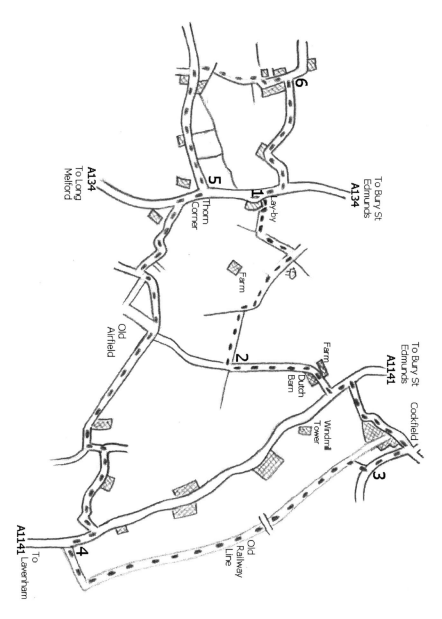

The perimeter runway is part of the disused Lavenham airfield. This was United States Airforce base 137, operational between March 1944 and August 1945. The 487th Bombardment Group flew 185 Missions and over 6000 separate sorties from here on bombing raids over Germany and occupied Europe, initially in Liberators and then Flying Fortresses before returning to the US at the end of the war.

9   Smithbrook Lane

$6^1/_4$ Miles   3 Hours

Park in the car park at Hartest. No toilets, local shops and pub the 'Crown'.

1   Turn right out of the car park entrance, uphill out of the village. After a third of a mile turn right at the signpost along the hedged farm track, Smithbrook Lane. Towards the top of the rise after the dip, turn left up the green farm track in front o a decorative brick wall.

2   Follow the field edge with the hedge to the right past a wire enclosure and bear right uphill. Turn left at the boundary with the hedge to the right, turn right at the signpost and keep general direction on obvious paths to the B1066 road.

3   Turn right for 300yds to the signpost and turn left along the right hand field edge, carry on past where the hedge stops to a marker post and follow the dyke right. Keep on the field edge turn left, right and left again up to the road.

4   Turn left, as the road swings left towards a farm turn right at a signpost and bear right then left uphill. Carry on to the marker post and bear right to the road; turn right along the road to the concrete sign.

5   Turn left to the hedge ahead; go down the right hand side of the left hand field and continue down the tree lined track. Join a farm track right/straight on to a marker post at a field boundary and turn right, follow the right hand field edge with the hedge to the right. Continue on the track to the right of the house.

6   Turn to the left at the hardcore road and right at the junction. Bear right at the marker post past the right hand side of the farm and right at the signpost beyond. Continue straight on through the hedge gap past the house to the road. Turn left along the road to the signpost at the white thatched house and go right.

7   Follow the left hand field edge through the boundary and turn right; keep going down the right hand field edge. Bear right through a narrow hedge gap and continue down the slope. Turn right over a sleeper bridge, follow the path through the trees and keep direction to the village green. Turn left and walk up the slope to the village hall and your vehicle in the car park to the rear.

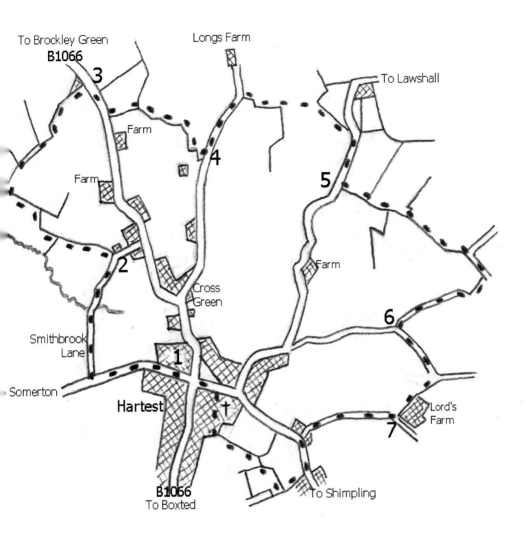

Hartest is a typical Suffolk village with an impressive church and chocolate box cottages lining the edges of a large village green. It is surrounded by acres of undulating farmland, sometimes bleak and windswept; broken up by scattered clumps of trees, isolated houses and farms often encircled by an ancient moat.

The church is the result of extensive rebuilding in the 1660's. The original tower, built in the 14th century, collapsed onto the church in 1650. The repairs and rebuilding cost the massive sum of £60.

23:H

10   Bull's Wood

5 Miles   2$\frac{1}{2}$ Hours

Find a parking space near the church in Cockfield, not a great deal of room but some space on the side of the road between the school and the main road. No facilities, shop on the main road going away from the A1141.

1   Start along the path next to the school car park, follow the arrowed direction along the left hand field edge. Turn left through the hedge gap at the marker post, keep direction through the boundary and bear right. Go through another boundary, cross the footbridge ahead and turn left with the dyke and the hedge on the left.

2   Continue on the track through the trees, over the hardcore farm road and the footbridge. Bear left over a smaller two sleeper footbridge, turn right with the dyke and follow it round the corner.

3   At the signpost turn right and cross the field in the arrowed direction, this field may be under cultivation but a track should be visible within any crop. Cross over the wide sleeper footbridge and the smaller one left, carry on along the field edge with the dyke to the left; bear left with the dyke and right in the corner. Keep direction over another two sleeper footbridge, bear right still on the field edge past the next more substantial footbridge up to the road.

4   Cross and maintain direction with the dyke still left; continue on this field edge which leads eventually to the road close to the pink house. Turn left and almost immediate right at the junction.

5   Follow the road for 200yds to the signpost and double back with the hedge to the right, keep on the field edge round to the left to complete the Z. Continue with the hedge on the right to the marker post and turn right over the footbridge; turn immediate left to get back to the original direction with the hedge to the left. Maintain this direction to the corner of Bull's Wood.

6   A choice here: go straight on to the far corner of the wood; or take the more interesting route through. Turn left along the field edge with the wood to the right; turn right over the footbridge at the marker post and left at the first junction. Bear right on the clear path through the wood (look for marker posts) to the far corner.

7   From the kissing gate, follow the farm road ahead with the hedge to the right through the farm buildings up to the road. Cross and bear left along the roadside path to the footpath sign, turn right and walk along the hedge lined path bearing left. Bear right down the right hand field edge and rejoin the outward path back to Cockfield and your vehicle.

23:H

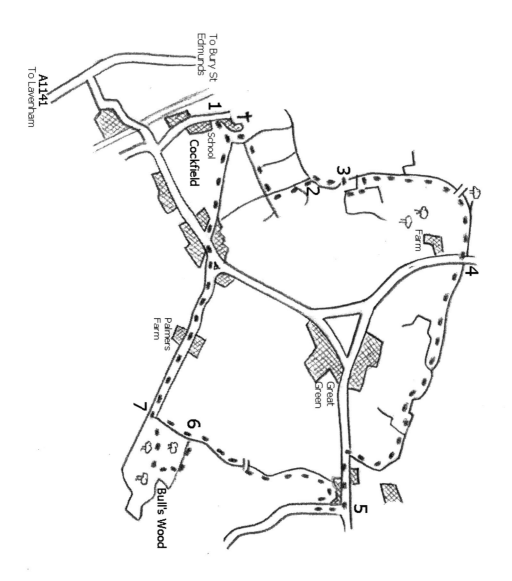

The village of Cockfield is spread over a vast area, a central nucleus close to the church is surrounded by a number of 'Greens'; Cross Green, Colchester Green, Great Green, Buttons Green and Windsor Green. Local folklore says that primroses will not grow within Cockfield; when the village suffered in the plague it was believed that the primroses also caught it and died.

The 'Walking Close to' Series

South and South West

Salisbury and Stonehenge
The New Forest (North and West)
Romsey and the Test Valley
Cheddar Gorge
Exmouth and East Devon
Corsham and Box (Wiltshire)
The Quantock Hills (West Somerset)
Blandford Forum (Dorset)
Chichester and the South Downs

Winchester and the South Downs
The New Forest (South and East)
The East Devon Coast
Glastonbury and the City of Wells
The Avon near Bath
The Avon near Chippenham (Wiltshire)
Shaftesbury (Dorset)
Bradford-on-Avon (Wiltshire)

East Anglia and Lincolnshire

The Nene near Peterborough
Lavenham (Suffolk)
The Nene Valley Railway near Wansford
The Nene near Oundle
The Great North Road near Stilton
Bury St Edmunds
Norfolk Broads (Northern Area)
Southwold and the Suffolk Coast
North West Norfolk (Hunstanton and Wells)
North Norfolk (Cromer and Sheringham)
The Lincolnshire Wolds (North)
The Stour near Sudbury (Suffolk)
Chelmsford
Epping Forest (Essex/North London)
The Colne near Colchester
Thetford Forest (Norfolk/Suffolk)
The Great Ouse in Huntingdonshire
The Torpel Way (Stamford to Peterborough)

Grafham Water (Huntingdonshire)
Dedham Vale (Suffolk/Essex)
The Cam and the Granta near Cambridge
Lincoln
The Welland near Stamford
The Isle of Ely
Norfolk Broads (Southern Area)
Aldeburgh, Snape and Thorpeness
Clare, Cavendish and Haverhill
Bourne and the Deepings
The Lincolnshire Wolds (South)
The Orwell near Ipswich
Stowmarket (Suffolk)
Hertford and the Lee Valley
Newmarket
The Great Ouse near King's Lynn
South Lincolnshire

Midlands

The Nene near Thrapston
The Nene near Wellingborough
The River Ise near Kettering
The Nene near Northampton
Rockingham Forest (Northamptonshire)
Daventry and North West Northamptonshire
Rugby
Stratford-upon-Avon
Rutland Water
Eye Brook near Uppingham
The Soar near Leicester
Lutterworth (Leicestershire)
The Vale of Belvoir (North Leicestershire)
Melton Mowbray
The Welland near Market Harborough
Banbury
South West Herefordshire

The Great Ouse near Bedford
Woburn Abbey (Bedfordshire)
Sherwood Forest
Pitsford Water (Northamptonshire)
The Thames near Oxford
The Trent near Nottingham
The Vale of White Horse
Henley-on-Thames
The River Pang (Reading/Newbury)
The Great Ouse north of Milton Keynes
The Cotswolds near Witney
The Malvern Hills
The Dukeries (Sherwood Forest)
The Severn near Worcester
Woodstock and Blenheim Palace
The Kennet near Newbury

Cumbria

Cartmel and Southern Lakeland